Play it Again

Suggestions for Drama

Sue Porter

Hodder & Stoughton

LONDON SYDNEY AUCKLAND TORONTO

British Library Cataloguing in Publication Data

Porter, Sue
  Play it again.
  1. Drama in education
  2. Improvisation (Acting)
  I. Title
  792'.028   PN3171

  ISBN 0 7131 0698 0

First published 1984
Reprinted 1985, 1990

Printed in Great Britain for the educational publishing division of
Hodder and Stoughton Ltd, Mill Road, Dunton Green, Sevenoaks, Kent
by Athenaeum Press Ltd, Newcastle upon Tyne.

Contents

Preface

Numbers in brackets indicate number of characters for which each situation is intended.

Preface

Play It Again contains 20 situations for drama, for groups of 2, 3 and 4 to improvise. It is divided into four thematic sections: 'Conflict', 'The Light of Truth' (involving many crises of conscience and questions of morality), 'Under Pressure' (involving reactions to emergencies) and 'A Change of View' (exploring the way in which our view of people can be modified by experience).

The book is designed so that pupils can work from it self-sufficiently. No explanation or preparation is required from the teacher – though of course follow-up work in the form of discussion and writing could easily evolve afterwards.

It is recommended that pupils attempt the situations for 2 characters to start with. Though work in pairs is often demanding, it is easier to organise than work in larger groups. Larger groups require a greater amount of patience and consideration. Situations involving 4 characters will therefore prove more accessible to pupils who are already experienced at work in pairs and threes.

Teachers should stress that drama improvisation is a process of give and take – of listening and responding as well as initiating. Pupils should be encouraged, in the 'Try it Again with a Twist' sections to re-examine the whole situation in the light of altered circumstances. Moreover, they may benefit, when playing it again, by swapping the parts around.

Each situation is also furnished with suggestions for discussion and for practical work afterwards.

S.P.

Conflict

1 Neither a Borrower Nor a Lender Be . . .

A Hey, there's this fantastic film on at the Plaza this week! It's that one with Sting in.

B Oh, great. Shall we go tomorrow night?

A Yeah. I'm supposed to go and see my Gran but I'll get out of it somehow.

B Bring her along! She's a Sting fan, isn't she?

A No, not really. She's more a Heavy Metal sort of Gran.

B Oh, there's just one thing, though . . .

A What?

B I've run out of cash. So could you lend me the money for the ticket?

A Well, I don't know, really . . .

B Just till the weekend? I can pay you back Saturday night.

A I don't suppose you remember . . . but I did actually lend you some two weeks ago.

B Did you? Oh God! I'm sorry! I completely forgot. How much was it?

A Three quid. It was the night we went to the disco.

B Oh yeah! Of course! Hey, that was a really naff disco, wasn't it? The D.J. was a right wimp.

A Yeah.

B How do you suppose he got to be a D.J.? Do you reckon it's easy? I quite fancy it myself.

A I don't know.

B Look, I'll pay you back. Don't worry. Tell you what – if you lend me two quid now that'll make it five. I'll pay you back Saturday, honestly.

A I'm not sure I can.

B Go on! Be a devil. You won't regret it. When I'm a disc-jockey and stinking rich you can stay on my yacht in the South of France.

Discuss

Discuss all the different ways you can think of in which money makes trouble between people. Try and work out some possible solutions to each problem. Think of the conflicts between parents and children, husbands and wives, employers and workers, brothers and sisters and friends.

The Plot Thickens

2 Characters:

A someone who manages their money well.
B someone who is always short of cash and borrows.

The Outline

B often borrows money from **A**, and promises to pay it back, but instead the debt slowly mounts up. Eventually **A**'s father loses his job, so **A** needs money and wants **B** to repay the debt. **B** has to work hard at various ways of earning the money. Their relationship is damaged by the strain.

A. You enjoy lending money to **B** at first. Why? When your father loses his job, your life has to change in many ways. How? Think of some details. How would you approach **B** with a view to getting your money back? What ideas would you suggest as ways for **B** to earn money to repay you?

B. What's your attitude to **A**: are you grateful for the loans, do they make you feel under an obligation? What's your reaction to the news about **A**'s father? How do you feel about having to do a lot of extra work to repay **A**? Did you, in fact, secretly believe that you never would have to pay it back? You feel angry with yourself. How might this spill over into your dealings with **A**?

Suggested story-line

1 **A** and **B** are at the fair. **B** soons runs out of money and **A** pays for everything.
2 **A** and **B** planning a holiday. **A** is very keen for **B** to go, and offers to lend a lot towards the cost of it.
3 **A** tells **B** that his/her father has lost his job, and that all the debts must be paid. They discuss ways in which this could be done.

4 **B**, exhausted by a hard day's gardening, is visited by **A** who wants some money. They are friendly: the tension remains under the surface at this stage.

5 **B**, even more tired out, goes to **A**'s house with more of the money, to find **A** watching TV. This time the tension explodes into a full-scale row.

Try it again with a twist

What if **B** was injured in the course of the extra work he/she was having to do?

Things to do

Collect all the songs you can find which are about money in some way. Listen to them and make a careful study of the different attitudes to money which they represent. What do you think is a healthy attitude to money? Make a list of the things that make you happy which can be bought with money, and the things that can't. Try and work out: can money buy a certain sort of happiness? What sort? Keep a record of all the money that passes through your hands, for a week. People are often rather secretive and shy about money. What might the reasons be? Interview an adult you know and ask them about their feelings about money. Has money ever made them angry? Hurt? Resentful? Why? Write a story entitled 'The Root of All Evil' about money.

2 A Helping Hand

B Shall I make you a cup of tea, then?

A Eh?

B I said, shall I make you a cup of tea!!

A Oh, aye. All right, love. That'll be nice.

B Where are the matches?

A You what?

B Matches! To light the gas! To boil the kettle!

A They're on that shelf.

B No, they're not.

A Aren't they? Well, bless me! Where've they disappeared to, then?

B When did you last have them?

A Well, I might have had a little smoke when I was watching TV.

B I'll go and see . . .

A They'll be on that little table!

B No, they're not there!

A Well, blow me down! Where did I put them? I'll forget me own head next.

B Perhaps I should go out and buy some more.

A Eh?

B I said, I'll go out and buy some more! From the corner shop! I won't be long!

A That's kind of you, love. Just a minute – I'll give you the money. Now, where did I put my purse? . . .

Discuss

Who's the oldest person you know? On what sort of occasions do you see them? What part does the old person play in the conversation? Why are we tempted to think of old people as being all alike? Why is this quite wrong? Think of examples from your own experience.

What happens to human beings as they grow older? What special needs do old people have? How are they cared for? Might there be better ways of caring for them? What can old people contribute to the community? How could this be organised?

The Plot Thickens

2 Characters:

A an old person

B a young person

The Outline

B wants to make some extra money to help the local swimming pool fund. **A** is a neighbour who is too old to do much gardening and housework nowadays. **B** offers to help out, but **A** is difficult, keeps interfering and criticising, and it's hard for **B** to keep cool and calm about it.

A. What are the irritating things about being old? What's your reaction to **B**? Maybe you feel a mixture of things at different moments: gratitude and jealousy, for example. In what ways does **B** irritate you? (Not being thorough? Being too clumsy? Trying to rush through work?)

B. You know **A** slightly already, but you don't really know your way around the house, and because **A** is getting a bit forgetful, things often aren't where they should be. What sort of jobs do you offer to do? What difficulties do you encounter? How do you cope with **A**'s criticisms?

Suggested story-line

1 **B** arrives and explains to **A** that he/she will do housework or gardening in aid of the fund.
2 They discuss what jobs might be done and decide which to do first. **B** starts work.
3 **A** watches and begins to criticise.
4 **B** tries to persuade **A** to relax and sit down by the fire and let **B** get on with things.
5 After **B** has managed to keep his/her temper for a long time,

finally it snaps. After the row, they make friends again and feel closer than before.

Try it again with a twist

What if **B** broke one of **A**'s most treasured possessions?

Things to do

Interview an old person about life when they were young. Ask them how people lived, and how different things were: streets, houses, countryside, methods of transport, the sort of jobs people did, heating and lighting, education, health, shops, money, communications, holidays, ways of behaving, leisure pursuits. Tape record the interview or make notes and then write it up as a magazine article and send it to your local newspaper – or club together with your friends to make a whole book of such interviews.

3   Happy Birthday

Jane's Diary

Saturday 3rd May. Woke up late. Really angry. Mum hadn't called me, though she pretended she had. My breakfast had gone cold and was really YUK! Nothing to wear as all my nice clothes were in the wash, so borrowed Mum's new tracksuit. It's the only decent thing she's got, and only because I nagged her into doing herself up a bit. I dashed out to meet Mandy and we went round the shops. Saw a fantastic pink-and-white striped leotard. Went home and tried to persuade Mum to lend me £10 to buy it, but it was really annoying, she was hoovering and she wouldn't even switch off. So I had to scream at her just to be heard. And even then she wouldn't lend me the money. It's not fair.

In the afternoon I decided to make some apple pies and I'd just got everything all laid out and was up to my elbows in flour when the phone rang. It was Tony Hudson asking me to go off to the Fair with him. Well, I just washed my hands and ran! We had a fantastic time and I won a goldfish. I'm going to call him Cyril.

Tony asked me to the disco so (after swooning) I dashed home for a bite to eat first and to get changed. Tea wasn't ready, and though Mum had finished off my pies, they were still in the oven so I couldn't sample them. So I just gobbled up most of a cake that was lying about cooling. Delicious! I had to practically hit Mum over the head with my goldfish bowl to get her to iron my new top and trousers in time for me to meet Tony at 7.

Dad gave me a lift to the bus stop, which was just as well as I could hardly walk with my new shoes. Dad also slipped me a tenner as I got out of the car and winked and said, 'Here you are, love, have a bit of fun while you're young.' Dad's a darling. Bopped all night with Tony till my feet gave way. He's a darling too.

Discuss

What does the diary extract above tell us about Jane, her mother and her father? If you could meet Jane in person, do you think you'd like her? Why? What would you be tempted to say to her about her home life?

The Plot Thickens

3 Characters
A a hardworked Mum
B a goodnatured but rather thoughtless Dad
C a son or daughter who take after Dad

The Outline

It's Mum's birthday soon. **B** and **C** discuss how to celebrate it. They argue and finally decide on a surprise birthday breakfast party. But they're not helping Mum in their day-to-day lives, so when the great day arrives, she's got a terrible headache through overwork.

A. Do you gladly slave away for your family, or do you resent their laziness? In what ways do they create work for you? Do you think you spoil them in some ways – in fact, don't you make yourself into a bit of a doormat, maybe?

B. You enjoy home life very much, and appreciate your wife, but you just don't notice how hard she works, and you assume that she enjoys waiting on you hand and foot. You adore your daughter/son though you think some of her/his clothes, ideas and friends are a bit too much!

C. You are always trying to liven up your mum's image, and get her out of her rather dowdy rut. But you're also quite prepared to let her wait on you when it suits you: in fact, you're rather lazy at times!

Suggested story-line

1   After dinner, Mum clears away. Dad and child discuss the forthcoming birthday (while Mum's washing up!)
2   **C** watches TV while Mum cleans up around him/her. **C** tries to get an idea of what Mum would like for her birthday.
3   Lunchtime approaches. **B** and **C** want different things to eat, so Mum's got a lot of extra cooking to do. While she's doing it, **B** and **C** finalise their plans for the surprise Birthday Breakfast.
4   The great day arrives. **B** and **C** get up and prepare the festive breakfast. Then they discover that Mum's got a terrible headache and can't even open her eyes.

Try it again with a twist

Suppose, instead of having a headache, Mum slipped and broke her leg . . . and wouldn't be able to do the housework for some weeks as a result . . .

Things to do

Be nice to your Mum, or whoever does the housework at home. Volunteer to do it *all* yourself for a whole weekend while they put their feet up! Give them a holiday, and give yourself a piece of education!

Collect all the descriptions you can find in books and songs and magazines about mothers, and make a Mum anthology.

4 The Tower of Babel

Dad	Foul! That was a foul! The ref. must be blinking blind!
Mum	Clear away all those records from the table, now, Kim – I want to lay the supper.
Kim	OK, OK. (*sings*) Dear little darlin' – don't shed no tear . . . No woman no cry, yeah . . .
Gran	What's that song you're singing, Kim?
Kim	It's Bob Marley, Gran. The late, the great, the Undisputed King of Reggae.
Gran	It reminds me of a tune we used to have in my young day – now what was it called . . .
Dad	Goal! Goal! A great goal! A fantastic goal! Did you see that, Kim?
Kim	No, Dad. I was trying to mend my trainers.
Gran	What *was* it called, now? It's on the tip of my tongue.
Dad	That was a fantastic piece of teamwork, the way they set that one up. Look, Kim – here it is again on the Action Replay.
Gran	That fellow used to sing it – you know, the one who used to sing with what's his name's Orchestra. They used to play at the Alhambra. Joyce!
Mum	Yes, Mum? Haven't you cleared that table yet, Kim?
Dad	Look at that footwork! Poetry in motion!
Kim	(*sings*) No woman no cry . . . dear little darlin' . . .

Gran What was his name, Joyce? The one who used to sing at the Alhambra?

Mum This place is a madhouse.

The Plot Thickens

4 Characters
A Mum, who's a teacher
B Dad, a sports fanatic
C a teenager crazy about music
D a talkative Grandpa/Grandma

The Outline

The home here is too crowded. Mum needs space to work in, but Dad loves watching noisy sports programmes on TV and the teenager needs somewhere quiet to practise music. To crown it all, Grandpa/Grandma has come to stay and loves a good old natter . . .

A. You work very hard at home and at your job, and you need peace and quiet to do your marking. You're the peacemaker in the house, but when you're tired you often get a bit short-tempered yourself – and then you feel guilty afterwards!

B. You live for watching sport on TV, and get very excited and carried away by it all. You are irritated by the talkative Grandpa/Grandma, and you feel that your child spends too much time on music and not enough on homework.

C. You love music and like to practise on your guitar (or piano) as much as possible. You don't get on very well with your Dad at times, you feel protective towards your mum, and you get on very well with Grandpa/Grandma.

D. You've come to stay for a while – you usually live alone, so you're keen to catch up on all the news. You like to talk about the old days, and also you've got a good eye for your family's faults and shortcomings.

Suggested story-line

1 The homecoming. **D** is already at home. **C** arrives, then **A**. They get the tea together.
2 **B** arrives. **C** is practising music, **A** is marking. **B** wants his tea, and to watch a football match on TV.
3 **C** talks to **D** about the problems of trying to find a bit of space and privacy – and maybe other problems, too.
4 **D** tries to talk to **A** (who's trying to do her marking) and **B** (who's deep in a football match on TV) about **C**'s problems.
5 **D** and **B** have an argument. **A** tries to make peace between them. Then someone notices that **C** is missing . . .

Try in again with a twist

What if **C** has actually run away from home to escape from all the pressures? How would the others react?

Things to do

Sit very still and listen to all the noises you can hear. Make a list of them.

Make a list of the pleasant noises in every day life, and the unpleasant ones.

Go to the library and find out all you can about Noise Abatement.

Write a murder story in which a noisy neighbour is mysteriously done to death.

5 Striking Camp

C Don't you think we ought to plan a route?
B Oh, no! That'll spoil everything. You don't want a bloody

timetable when you're on holiday. You want to get up in the morning, pack up the tent, jump on your bike, and go off where the mood takes you.

C But what if the mood doesn't take you? Or what if we disagree?

B Don't be daft! We won't disagree!

D But shouldn't we at least get a list of camping sites from the Tourist Board or something?

B Camp sites! We're not going anywhere near camp sites!

C Where are we going, then?

B We camp in the wild. Under a tree. In a field. Wherever we feel like it.

D But farmers can get narked if you just camp on their land without permission.

B Well, so we get permission, don't we, dumbo?

C What about, well . . . washing, and lavatories, and all that?

B Stone me! You'll be wanting TV and a pool table next! What's the point of going camping unless you're actually surrounded by Nature?

D Yeah, but, well, Chris has got a point, though. What about washing and stuff?

B Streams. And rivers. Nature's bathroom.

D I don't suppose Nature actually lays it on hot and cold, though, does she?

Discuss

A lot of people enjoy holidays in the countryside more than being at the beach. Why do they like it so much, do you think? Discuss the conflicts that can arise between holidaymakers and country people. Why are summer visitors important to the countryfolk? How do you think the holiday business might have changed the countryside? In what ways might we try to preserve the best of the countryside? Would you prefer to live in the city or the country? Think of all the advantages of each, make a list of them, and try to assess their importance.

The Plot Thickens

4 Characters
A a farmer

B an experienced camper who like wild places
C an inexperienced, nervous camper
D a younger friend of **B** and **C**

The Outline

The three campers argue about where to set up camp. **B** wants adventure; **C** wants to be safe; **D** is influenced by **B** but is also easily scared. They camp on farm land, but the farmer doesn't get on very well with them and the episode ends in their being seen off the land.

A. You don't mind campers on your land, but at the moment you've got a lot of worries on your mind and you're rather short-tempered. You don't suffer fools gladly and you're not too impressed with these three friends.

B. You hate official camp sites. Your aim is to be close to nature. What sort of things do you like about life in the wild? What is your attitude to **D**? Maybe you start out feeling protective but become increasingly impatient.

C. You're very nervous. This is your first night under canvas. But what are you nervous of? And do you have complete faith in **B** – or do you feel he/she is a bit reckless at times? What's more, maybe you feel responsible for the younger one – **D**.

D. You're very excited about this holiday and determined to enjoy yourself. Like **C**, you're inexperienced but you're ready for anything. In fact you tend to over-react and let your imagination run away with you at times.

Suggested story-line

1 The group discusses where to pitch camp. **C** wants an official camp-site; **B** won't hear of it.
2 They find a farm and approach **A**, who give them permission to pitch their tents.
3 In the middle of the night the farmer hears strange noises and goes out into the field to investigate. He scares **C** to death, but **B** just thinks it's a great joke.
4 **D** leaves a gate open. A lot of cows get out and the farmer is furious. He tells the campers to get off his land.

5   The three friends are now deeply divided. **B** wants to camp in the woods; **C** wants to go home.

Try it again with a twist

Suppose **D** became ill – how would **B** and **C** react? And how might the farmer help, despite being so angry?

Things to do

Go to the library and ask for books about the countryside, especially the countryside as it was in the past. Look at *Cider with Rosie* by Laurie Lee, *Lark Rise to Candleford* by Flora Thompson, and any book by George Ewart Evans.

Try and find out how the countryside has changed in the past 100 years, and how it is still changing.

Make a huge collage of a country landscape, using details cut from magazines, advertisements, etc.

Take a pad and pencil to the nearest park, garden or stretch of countryside and try to sketch some of the very simple forms of nature: a snail's shell, a clover flower, a twig, a pine cone, a pebble. Make a collection of such objects for your bedroom windowsill. Try and work out how you might use the objects to create some kind of sculpture.

Borrow from the library a book which teaches you how to identify trees, and then go round your neighbourhood and work out what your local trees are. Get to know them and find out what they do at different seasons.

Write an account by a town dweller of a trip to the countryside to stay with some cousins. Then write an account of the same visit, but from the point of view of one of the cousins.

The Light of Truth

1   Mystery Voices

A   Hillfield 7311.
B   Hello?
A   Hello? Who is it?
B   Never mind who I am.
A   What?
B   I know who you are. I've been watching you.
A   Who are you?
B   Never mind that. I'm warning you. You've got it coming to you.
A   What do you mean?
B   Just watch your step. That's all. Just watch your step. Because if you're not very careful . . .
A   What?
B   You could fall into a thundering great bowl of custard.

The Plot Thickens

2 Characters:
A   a mischievous practical joker
B   A's best friend

The Outline

A and **B** are bored in the school holidays. One day **A** rings **B** up, puts on a different voice and scares **B** a lot. Later they both find it fun to make some anonymous phone calls – some silly, some scary. Then they hear that one of their victims is so terrified that he/she nearly has a nervous breakdown. **B** wants to own up and make amends, but **A** thinks they should lie low.

A.   You enjoy putting on funny voices, playing tricks, and in general being the life and soul of the party. You've always thought that **B** was a great friend and supporter, but when **B** wants to own up to the phone calls you feel betrayed.

B.   You enjoy making the phone calls, though you prefer them to be silly rather than threatening. But the news about your victim's near nervous breakdown really upsets you and changes your whole attitude.

Suggested story-line

1   **A** phones **B** and pretends to be someone else, for a joke.
2   Next day, **A** reveals it was him/her.
3   **A** and **B** make some calls together.
4   **B**, having heard about their victim's nervous breakdown, tells **A** and says they must own up.
5   **A** disagrees – accuses **B** of being cowardly. A major row blows up.

Try it again with a twist

What if, to try and keep **B** quiet, **A** threatens him/her – and seems to mean it?

Discuss

One of these friends is a strong personality, the other one follows the lead. Do you think all relationships are in some way a power struggle, with both partners competing for control? How does this develop? Do you have any friends who dominate you, who might be able to persuade you to do something against your wishes or judgement? Has this ever happened in the past? How do some people manage to get this kind of power? Are there people whom you know you can wind around your little finger? Why is it so hard to stand up against people with strong personalities?

Think and Write

Guilt is a terrible feeling, and we've nearly all had experience of it. Try and remember a time when you've felt very guilty about something, and write an account of it. When you've done something wrong, what is the best way of putting it right? Think about crimes being committed and the criminals being punished. Why do we punish people? Are there several reasons? What are they? Which are the most important, in your opinion?
   Imagine a young man has broken into an old woman's flat and

stolen her life's savings. Write down his account of the theft, and then write about it from her point of view. Lastly, write down your own ideas about how your think he should best be punished, considering all these possibilities:

corporal punishment (i.e. beating)
imprisonment in solitary confinement
useful work in prison
useful work and education
having to meet his victim face to face and talk to her about how his crime has affected her.

2 The Tangled Web

Gary's Diary

Sunday 24th October

Had an amazing dream last night. Dreamt I was playing in a Rock Band on a tour of the States. The crowds were incredible, and all these girls were throwing themselves at me! I was really brassed off when I woke up and found myself in my smelly little bedroom as usual.

Not a very pleasant morning. Dad had been down the boozer last night and he was sitting about like a bear with a sore head. Mum had her curlers in and she was chain-smoking as usual. Sharon painted her nails all through breakfast and what with the pong of the nail varnish and the cigarette smoke I could hardly face my egg and bacon.

I went for a run in the park this afternoon and saw the most beautiful girl. She was wearing a pink tracksuit and she was jogging past the bird cages. The mynah bird didn't half whistle and I don't blame him! She had lovely chestnut hair and she looked really fantastic. The trouble is, I could see she was right out of my class. A girl like that would never be interested in me – not in a million years.

Discuss

What do you think Gary means when he writes in his diary that he thinks the girl in the park is 'right out of his class'? What sort of things go to make up 'class' nowadays? What sort of life might the girl lead, and how would it differ from Gary's life? (Consider the area she might live in, her house, her parents' jobs, her possessions, her behaviour.) What difficulties would she and Gary face if they did fall in love?

Other things besides class can cause division and difficulty between friends, lovers and marriage partners. Race and religion can divide people, too. Think of some examples. If friends or lovers were divided by race or religion, how might they try to organise their lives to get round some of the difficulties?

The Plot Thickens

3 Characters:
A   a new boy/girl at school
B   his/her mother
C   the friend **A** makes at the new school

The Outline

A and **B** move to a new area. **A** makes a friend at school and begins tell him/her all sorts of fantasies about **A**'s home life. Then **A**'s mum invites the new friend home to tea and the truth – that **A**'s home is very ordinary – is all too clear.

A.   You feel a bit insecure in your new school, and maybe that's why you invent all sorts of things to impress your friend. What sort of things do you fantasise about? That your parents are rich or famous? How might you try and stop **C** from coming to tea?

B.   You're anxious that moving house may disturb your child and make it difficult for her/him to make new friends. So you encourage the signs that **A** is getting on well with **C**, and you're very keen to meet **C** – hence the tea invitation.

C. You're very impressed by your new friend, and believe everything **A** tells you. You've always trusted people in the past and don't see why you should stop now.

Suggested story-line

1 **A** and **B** having breakfast, the first morning of **A**'s new school term.
2 **A** meets **C** and they get talking. They like each other, but for some reason **A** starts to tell lies.
3 **A** goes home and tells mum about the first day and about **C**.
4 Mum rings up **C**'s mum and invites **C** to tea – despite objections from **A**.
5 **A** tries to stop **C** from coming to tea by all sorts of desperate manoeuvres next day at school.
6 **C** comes to tea, and tells **B** the lies that **A** has told.

Try it again with a twist

Suppose **B** didn't spill the beans, but behaved with great restraint . . . imagine the next private conversation between **A** and **C** . . .

Things to do

Fantasy and daydream are harmless, and probably necessary to all of us in moderation. It's only when we begin to confuse the fantasy with reality that things get out of hand. So exercise your fantasies in a pleasant and creative way.

Make a collage which includes some of the different fantasies you have: your ideal holiday, your dream house, your favourite landscapes, etc. Use old photographs of yourself, pictures cut out from magazines etc.

Keep a dream diary by your bedside. Every day when you first wake up, immediately write down the dream you've just had before you forget it. If you enjoy drawing and painting, illustrate it.

3   Under the Influence

A   Hello!

B   Oh, so you're home at last! And where do you think you've been?

A   Nowhere much. I went down the rec. with Tony.

B   That's not what I heard.

A   Eh?

B   It may interest you to know that I received a phone call while you were out.

A   What about?

B   From that Mr Rogers who lives down Wheelwright Lane. He saw you and Tony stealing apples off his tree.

A   We did not! What a cheek! We were miles away!

B   He recognised you. He even described the T-shirt you're wearing. Yes – that one.

A   Oh well, we were only having a bit of fun. It was only apple-scrumping. We only had a couple each. There's no need to get steamed up about it.

B   Oh, isn't there? Well Mr Rogers said that when you were running away you broke a whole section of his fence down. He reckons you did at least £30 worth of damage.

A   The old liar! We never touched his fence. It was broken already.

B   Well, that's what he said. Don't ask me which of you is lying. All I know is, when it comes to lying, you've got an unbeatable track record.

A   Oh, God. You won't even believe your own flesh and blood.

B   I *especially* won't believe my own flesh and blood. That thirty pounds has got to be paid – and you're the one who's going to pay it.

A   Oh, no! That bloody Tony! I'll kill him.

B   I always said that Tony would get you into trouble one day.

Discuss

You might think that apple-scrumping is just a bit of fun. All young people like to let off steam now and then. But sometimes it backfires and other people suffer. Have you ever caused pain or bother to other people without realising it? How did it make you feel? What's the best way of making it up to people afterwards?

The Plot Thickens

3 Characters:

A boy/girl
B A's mother
C A's best friend

The Outline

A's mother disapproves of **C** as a friend for her child. She feels that **C** is a bad influence. The two friends go apple-scrumping but the owner sees them and tells the mother. She forbids her child to see the friend again.

A. You have fun with **C** and can't understand why your mother disapproves. In fact, it's usually you who has the ideas and takes the lead, and you're certainly eager to take part in anything risky.

B. Why do you disapprove of **C**? Is it that you can't possibly believe your own child would ever do anything wrong? You're a nervous person and imagine trouble even where there isn't any.

C. You like **A** very much but you know **A**'s mother doesn't like you. You know this is unfair but you just accept it: you have a relaxed, easy-going attitude to life, and are quite prepared to follow **A**'s lead.

Suggested story-line

1   **A** and **B** are having tea. **B** asks **A** about what's happened during the day. **A** mentions **C**, and Mum shows her disapproval.
2   **A** and **C** go apple-scrumping – but are seen by the owner.
3   When **A** gets home, Mum is waiting and angry – she's been

phoned by the owner who recognised **A** and **C**.

4 **B** orders **A** not to see **C** any more. A fierce argument follows.
5 **A** has to tell **C** about Mum's reaction.

Try it again with a twist

Suppose **A** and **C** instead of apple-scrumping, steal a car and crash it – and it was all **A**'s idea . . .

Things to do

Write a play in three parts.

Part 1: Carol meets a boy called Darren who's been to an Approved School, but is now a skilled carpenter and a reformed character. She tells her Mum about it and her Mum is doubtful but willing to give him a chance.

Part 2: Carol's Mum tells her Dad about it. He explodes and orders Carol to end the relationship. Carol refuses. When they're alone, Carol and her Mum hatch a plot to ask Darren to tea the next day, without Dad knowing.

Part 3: The Tea. Dad arrives late and Darren has already made a good impression on Carol's Mum. At first Dad is very angry that it's all been set up behind his back, but later he cools down, gets to know Darren and decides he likes him after all.

4 A Day Off

A You know that Maths Test this afternoon?
B Oh, Gawd – don't remind me.
A Well, let's get out of it.

B What do you mean? How can we?

A Skive off.

B Skive off! You must be mad! Everybody knows we're here today.

A Old Skinner doesn't know. And he never notices anything anyway. I don't think he can even see out of those old specs of his.

B Someone would be bound to notice.

A No they won't. There's hardly anybody from our form in our maths set anyway. And if they say anything tomorrow, we can say you felt ill so I took you home.

B You sound very experienced! Ever done this sort of thing before?

A Oh, yeah. Ever so many times. I go down town and hang around the shops. Once I spent the whole afternoon in Dino's drinking Espressos.

B And you never got caught?

A Never. This school's so big, nobody notices. You just nip out at lunchtime in the general throng, and you don't come back. Even if the teacher takes the register at the beginning of the afternoon class, they never check up on you. You can say you went to the dentist and they never ask to see a letter or anything. Go on! We can go and play the video games at Wakefield's.

B Oh, all right.

The Plot Thickens

3 Characters:

A someone who often skives off school

B A's friend

C B's mother/father

The Outline

A persuades **B** that it's fun to skive off from school and that there's no chance of their being caught. They spend the day in town, in cafes and the park. **B** becomes more and more nervous and when she/he gets home, confesses all.

A. What's your attitude to school? Pretty negative? Are you trying to impress **B**? Maybe you even thrive on the dangers of skiving – you like to show off your cool nerve. What is it you like about **B**? How would you persuade **B** to join you in your day off?

B.   **A** persuades you to skive, but you're nervous, convinced that you'll be seen or caught. You only manage to enjoy yourself now and then. Do you feel much better after you've told all to Mum/Dad?

C.   What's your reaction to **B**'s behaviour? Though you're a gentle and forgiving parent, you're probably shocked that **B** should be so easily influenced – and you certainly want to question **B** not only about this, but about **A** in general.

Suggested story-line

1   **A** and **B** on the bus on the way to school. **A** persuades **B** to skive off.
2   They go round the shops and sit in a cafe. **B** is often nervous, **A** tries to laugh it off.
3   **B** goes home, and **C** askes about the day at school. At first **B** tries to lie but gets flustered.
4   **B** breaks down and tells **C** everything. **C** asks a lot of questions about **A**, whom he/she's never met.
5   **B** tells **A** (next day) that **C** knows about it.

Try it again with a twist

Suppose that when **A** and **B** are going round the shops they actually bump into **C**?

Discuss

One of the reasons people get away with skiving is that schools are so big nowadays. Discuss the pros and cons of
   Only children versus large families
   Huge comprehensive schools versus small local village
      schools.
   Big hotels versus small bed-and-breakfast places
   Large institutions versus the independent self-employed man
      or woman.
   Mass produced goods versus craftsman-designed objects.
      (e.g. pottery, furniture, fabrics, etc.)

Things to do

Devise a questionnaire to be filled in (anonymously!) by your friends and classmates, asking them if they have ever skived, or committed other minor crimes against school rules. Make room on the questionnaire form for them to give their opinion about the way the school is run, how it could be improved etc.

Write a report based on the findings of the questionnaire. Draw up a series of school rules for your own ideal school. Make the architectural drawings and plans for your ideal school, giving it the best possible environment and assuming that money is no object.

5 Shopped

15 Primrose Drive
Hayfield
Avon.
30th July

Dear Steve,

I'm sorry I can't come to the disco with you on Friday after all. Something really awful has happened. Mum came home in tears today. She'd been in the local supermarket and apparently the Store Detective caught her putting some things in her bag instead of in the wire basket! Mum's absolutely desperate. She says she's no idea why she did it, in fact, she can't even remember doing it. She says she was miles away at the time. She was thinking about Dad losing his job – you know his firm's closing down next month and everybody's going to lose their jobs.

Ever since we knew about it, Mum's kept saying, 'However are we going to manage when your Dad's unemployed?' It's been really preying on her mind. Apparently we'll be all right for money for a while as Dad will get a fairly big redundancy payment – a sort of golden handshake. When Mum started getting so nervous about it she went to the doctor and he gave her some tranquillisers. She's been ever so absent-minded and dopey ever since and I'm sure that's why she took those things in the supermarket.

Anyway, I don't want to leave her alone tomorrow night because it's Dad's night for his cricket match, and Kev's away on a course. She's ever so upset at the moment and so we're trying to make sure that there's always someone here to chat and take her mind off things. Sorry about the disco. Next week, maybe?

Lots of love,
Janice.

Discuss

What hidden problems are revealed by Janice's Mum's shoplifting? Do you think the family is responding well to the crisis? How might other, less sympathetic families have reacted?

Janice's Mum's chief worry was the fact that her husband would soon lose his job. Unemployment is a very big problem nowadays. What are some of the reasons for the rise in unemployment, do you think? How have our lives changed in, say, the last 100 years? Think about machines and their place in our lives – in the house as well as outside and in industry. The most recent and sophisticated machines are of course computers. How might computers further change our lives in the next 50 years?

The Plot Thickens

3 Characters:
A   a supermarket supervisor
B   a young person, new to the job
C   B's friend's mother

The Outline

B has managed to get a job at a supermarket. **A** shows **B** the ropes, and **B** is quick to learn: they get on well. Then one day **B** notices somebody shoplifting. **B** recognises the shoplifter – it's the mother of **B**'s best friend.

A. You're proud of your efficiency and not sure this new employee is going to be up to scratch. So at first you're quite tough with **B**. But **B** impresses you, and you're very pleased with his/her progress.

B You like your new job, though you're nervous at first. But you get on well with **A** and soon you're really enjoying yourself there. When you recognise **C** shoplifting, you're placed in a real dilemma. Finally, you tell **A**.

C. You know and like **B**. You're a bit overworked and you've been forgetful lately. You've also got problems with money and a large family to feed. You've never shoplifted before.

Suggested story-line

1   **B**'s first day at the supermarket. **A** shows **B** around, explains about marking prices, checking stock etc.
2   A few days later. **B** by now at home and efficient at the job. **A** warns **B** about shoplifters.
3   **B** sees **C** shoplifting, and after hesitating, tells **A**.
4   **A** takes **C** to the office and questions her – finally has to call in **B** as a witness. **C** is very ashamed and confused and tells conflicting stories.
5   **C** confronts **B**. **B** persuades **A** not to call the police.

Try it again with a twist

Suppose **B** hadn't told **A**? What would happen when **A** found stock missing? Might **B** try to see **C** privately about it?

Things to do

Janice's Mum was very worried about unemployment. It seems that in the future many more people will be unemployed. Some people think this is not a disaster but a great opportunity, and that we should enjoy the chances of more leisure to spend our time in sport, painting, music, drama, the arts, gardening, exploring, sailing, etc. Design a timetable for a school of the future in which children would be educated for leisure only.

What problems, if any, might arise in such a world? Would the advantages outweigh the disadvantages? Compose the front page of a newspaper of the future, with news stories showing the way the world has changed since work ceased to rule people's lives.

Under Pressure

1   Con Man

M   Well, we must be off now, love. Are you sure you'll be all right?

A   Yeah. Of course I will.

M   I've left you a pie for tonight. It's wrapped up in foil, in the fridge. All you have to do is heat up the oven for 10 minutes or so – I've written all the instructions down on the . . .

A   I know. I know, Mum. I saw them. It's all right. Don't fuss.

M   I'm not fussing! I'm just trying to make sure you're all right. You know what you're like. Your head's like a sieve.

A   No it isn't! I can manage perfectly well. There's no need to go on.

M   Don't forget to lock all the doors and windows tonight.

A   All right, all right.

M   And I've left a note of our phone number in case you need to get in touch with us.

A   OK.

M   And whatever you do don't let anybody in.

A   Honestly, Mum! Do you think I'm that stupid?

The Plot Thickens

2 Characters:

A   someone left alone in the house while their parents are out

B   a person who calls and says he/she is a buyer of antique furniture

The Outline

A is left alone and feels quite confident about being able to deal with things while the parents are away for the weekend. Then there's a ring at the door: **B** is an extremely persuasive person who seems perfectly harmless, and just wants to look around the house to see if there's any antique furniture they might be interested in selling . . .

A. You're a fairly relaxed and easy-going sort of person, not easily made nervous. You reckon you can tell who's straight and who's a crook. But once **B** is inside the house you start to feel a bit more anxious. What sort of things might you try to use to get **B** to go away?

B. Of course, you're a criminal: you've come to see if there's any good furniture there so you can break in later. You know **A**'s parents have gone away and, sure enough, there are lots of very valuable things all over the place. You might try to get **A** to go away for a little while so you can steal the stuff immediately: you might try to get away with it now under **A**'s nose . . .

Suggested story-line

1   **B** comes to the door. **A** answers it and keeps **B** talking on doorstep for a while. **B** talks about all sorts of things, asks **A** what he/she's doing at school, etc, and finally is so nice that **A** lets him/her in.
2   **B** goes round the house looking for valuables. At the same time **B** tries to keep talking to reassure **A**.
3   **A** begins to feel anxious and tries to get rid of **B**, at first making excuses, but gradually becoming more desperate.
4   Finally **A** demands that **B** goes, but instead **B** ties **A** up and decides to do the robbery there and then.

Try it again with a twist

Suppose that instead of being a thief, **B** is a kidnapper, and **A** is the child of rich parents . . .

Discuss

Crime is on the increase these days. What do you think could be done by each family to make it harder for thieves to break in? Why might the crime rate be higher in the cities than in the country?

Children are often the victims of crime. Do you think they are always well enough protected against criminals? What could be done to improve this?

Things to do

Design some really crazy burglar alarms!

Train yourself to be a private detective. Notice people's faces, car number plates, suspicious behaviour, the time of day when things happen. (Don't intervene if you ever see an actual crime being committed, though. It's much better to stay in the background and try and remember as many details as you can.)

Play an observation game with a friend. In a given time (say, 10 minutes) you should both see how many details you notice in a typical street. After 10 minutes have elapsed, you both start to write down as many things as you can remember about what happened in those ten minutes. Compare notes afterwards and see if you've noticed the same things. Another observation game: open any book and read the first few lines over to yourself a couple of times. Look at them really hard and try to memorise them. Then close the book, pick up a pen and see how much of those first few lines you can manage to write down from memory.

2 Castaways

A Hullo?
B Jasmine Hill 221?
A Hello! Is that Ben?
B Yeah. Who's that? It's surely not – it's not Al, is it?
A That's right. What a memory! You never forget a voice, eh?
B Well, not your voice, mate. You always did sound like a rusty gate.

A Thanks a bunch! I can see you're still your old self. How's life treating you?

B Oh, so so. Not so bad. Getting a bit fat and lazy nowadays, you know.

A Marriage agrees with you, eh?

B Sure.

A Sheila's a great cook, I remember. And you've got kids now.

B Yeah. Two. The older one is four.

A So – you're weighed down with the old family responsibilities, then, Ben?

B Well – sort of.

A So I don't suppose you'd be interested in any little proposition I might want to make?

B What sort of proposition, exactly?

A Well . . . you know, I was thinking of making another of my little sailing trips quite soon, and I sort of wondered . . . well, if you'd be interested in coming along again as Mate.

B Oh no, sorry, Al, but it's absolutely out of the question. It's all right for you single geezers – fancy free. No responsibilities . . . Where are you thinking of going?

A This time I thought I'd go for a big one. Round the world.

B Round the world! Stroll on down!

The Plot Thickens

2 Characters:

A a round-the-world yachtsman

B the first mate

The Outline

Two friends are on a round-the-world yacht race when a storm blows up and they are wrecked on a desert island. At first **B** is despondent and homesick, but the other tries to persuade **B** that it could be fun. They have to build a shelter, feed themselves, and possibly build a boat to try and escape in . . .

A. You're an optimist, and you love danger. So when you're wrecked on the island you just feel it's a chance to explore and try and be resourceful. You have to try and cheer **B** up – what ways would you try? Getting **B** to do things? Cracking jokes?

35

B.   You're rather a nervous person and the shipwreck is a tremendous shock to you. Unlike **A**, who's single, you've got a family waiting for you back home, and you're beginning to despair of ever seeing them again. What's more, you regard the shipwreck as to some extent **A**'s fault as you feel the boat wasn't well-equipped enough.

Suggested story-line

1   **A** and **B** on board their yacht. A storm warning comes through on the radio and soon afterwards a gale blows up. They are wrecked.
2   They build a shelter on the island.
3   **A** makes a bow and arrow and goes hunting. **B** builds a fire. But **B** is becoming depressed.
4   **B** loses his/her nerve and provokes a row. The loneliness of the place and their desperate plight terrify **B**.
5   **A** manages to calm **B** down and they build a boat to try and escape . . .

Try it again with a twist

Suppose that they find gold on the island – and **A** wants it all to him/herself . . .

Discuss

On a desert island you would soon become aware of all the ways in which our normal daily lives have become extremely protected and cushioned from reality and from Nature in the raw. Think of your daily life and work out how every single thing you do on an ordinary day would be different if you were on a desert island. Try and think of all the ways in which your day-to-day existence is made easier by sophisticated machinery and products of industry. What attractions nevertheless does life on a desert island provide? What aspects of modern Western life would you be glad to escape from, and why?

Things to do

Draw a map of your ideal desert island. Imagine you have been wrecked there and write a diary of your adventures. You might meet and get to know some natives after a while.

Go to your library and ask for *Robinson Crusoe* by Daniel Defoe and *Lord of the Flies* by Willian Golding. They are both books about being stranded on a desert island. Make a list of the 8 records you'd take with you on *Desert Island Discs*!

3   Where there's smoke . .

Fran's Diary

Friday 18th March

God, I feel really terrible. This must be the worst day of my life. Mum went out tonight to see Auntie Kath leaving me in charge of Terry. I've babysat for him dozens of times before and in fact I felt a bit fed up because I really wanted to go to the disco with Gina. Still, I knew it was no use arguing. So I just sat down by the phone and made a lot of calls instead. Halfway through, Terry came in and asked me to make him some chips. I told him to shove off and stop pestering me, and he wandered off.

The next thing I knew, I heard this scream and crash. I dashed into the kitchen and Terry was roaring his head off and holding his arm, and the chip pan was on fire. My mind went sort of into overdrive and somehow I remembered that you're not supposed to try and carry the pan outdoors or throw water on it. You're meant to smother it. So I grabbed Dad's old motor-cycle jacket off the kitchen door and threw it over the pan. The flames died down, thank God, and the fire was out in a couple of minutes, although it made a right mess of the wall and the ceiling above the cooker.

But I didn't have time to think about that, because Terry was screaming blue murder. I didn't know what to do so I just ran and rang Auntie Kath and she said to wrap his arm in a clean tea towel and Mum would be right over. Well soon Mum was here, the ambulance came and she and Terry went off to hospital. I'm writing this waiting for them to come home. I dread what Mum's going to say. I can't bear the thought that Terry got hurt because of me. I think I'm going to die of shame . . .

Discuss

What would your reaction be if you were Fran's Mum? What would you say to Fran when you came back from the hospital? In general, do you think parents should be stricter or more tolerant? If you were a parent, what sort of rules or guide lines would you lay down for your children?

The Plot Thickens

3 Characters:
A   a parent
B   older child
C   younger child

The Outline

A goes out for the evening, leaving **B** in charge of **C**. **B** is very busy watching TV and telephoning friends, and when **C** asks **B** to make some chips, **B** ignores **C**. So **C** tries to do it his/herself, and the chip-pan catches fire. **B** manages to put the fire out, but **C** is burnt.

A.   Why do you need to go out? Where are you going? You trust **B**, but you also know that **B** is rather absent-minded and apt to ignore **C**, so you deliver a pep-talk before you go.

B.   You think **C** is sweet at times, but at other times **C**'s no more than a little pest. You particularly want to talk to a lot of friends on the phone this evening because you've just got back from holiday and you want to talk about the fantastic time you had.

C.   You like **B** very much and wish **B** would find more time for you. But when **B** is so busy you decide to make the chips yourself. You can't understand why the chip-pan catches fire and try and pick it up and run outside with it. You get burnt and drop it.

Suggested story-line

1   Mum goes out, warning **B** to look after **C** and telling **C** to behave. **B** starts phoning friends, **C** hangs about and pesters.
2   **C** wants chips; **B** is too busy so **C** goes off and does it by her/himself. The pan catches fire; **C** screams.
3   **C** tries to carry pan outside, drops it, is burnt. **B** puts fire out by smothering it with rug (mum's best rug!)
4   **B** tries to soothe the badly-hurt **C** and phones auntie, where mum has gone, to call for help.
5   Mum rushes home, calls the ambulance, and **C** is taken care of. Then Mum turns her attention to **B** . . .

Try it again with a twist

Suppose **C** didn't want chips, but instead took the chance, while **B** was phoning his/her friends, to run away from home . . .

Things to do

Draw a plan of your home, showing all the things in it that could be a possible source of danger to a small child. Design an ideal 'safety first' home in which all the possible dangers are done away with.

4   Jack Fell Down

A   OK, how's breakfast shaping up?
B   The kettle's boiling! Watch out!
A   OK, OK, don't get your knickers in a twist.
C   It's all right, I'll make the coffee.

A Isn't it great, camping and having breakfast in the open air?
C Fantastic! Just look at that view! And I'm so hungry! I could eat a horse.
A Well, there's a donkey in that field over there – if you think you could get it in the frying pan.
B Mind you don't spill that coffee! You nearly sat on it!
C It doesn't matter if it does spill on the grass, does it?
A Where do you want to go today, for our walk?
C I don't know. Get the map out and have a look.
B Right. It looks as if there's a nice walk over in that direction – beyond that church spire. There's a hill. Oh! there's a sort of swamp down in the valley, though, we'll have to be careful.
C A swamp? We don't get swamps in England.
A You've been watching too many Westerns.
B It looks a bit far, though.
C What? Just as far as that hill? Don't be such a wimp – it's nothing. I bet it's not even four miles.
B It looks further on the map.
A Let's have a look. No, that's nothing. We'll get there before lunch.
B We must be careful not to get blisters, though.
C I won't get blisters! I wore these boots in long before last Easter.
A Nor will I.
B I think I'll take some plasters, though – just in case.

Discuss

'Two's company, three's a crowd.' Do you agree? Sometimes people can get on each other's nerves more than ever on holiday. Why is this? Can you think of ways of avoiding it? What's the best thing to do if you find yourself getting really irritated by somebody? What sort of holidays do you most enjoy? What, for you, is the thing that could most easily spoil your enjoyment?

The Plot Thickens

3 Characters:
A a calm, relaxed person
B a friend who tends to panic and is nervous
C another friend, rather a clumsy person

The Outline

Three friends go for a walk up a hill. It's very hot, and the hill's very steep. At the top of the hill, **C** twists an ankle and faints. **B** panics and doesn't know what to do; **A** stays calmer and sorts the situation out.

A   You're a fairly quiet and relaxed person. You like walking, and you've got a camera which you use a lot. When **C** faints, you find that **B** panicking causes almost as much of a problem as **C**! You've got no first aid training but you can see that it will be best for one of you to stay with **C** and one go for help. The trouble is, both you and **B** want to stay with **C**.

B   You're excitable and nervous. You really enjoy life, and love the view from the hill, the exercise, and the idea of going on lots more walks. But when **C** faints, you're terrified. How on earth are you and **A** going to get **C** back down to the road? It's at least a mile away.

C   You're really enjoying yourself until you twist your ankle: then you're in quite a lot of pain. You find **B**'s fussing very irritating and you depend on **A** to get you out of this jam.

Suggested story-line

1   **A**, **B** and **C** are walking up the hill, enjoying themselves.
2   **C** slips and twists an ankle and faints. **B** panics.
3   **C** comes round again, but is in great pain and can't stand.
4   **B** and **A** argue what to do. **A** wants to stay with **C** but **B** insists that he/she should. Reluctantly **A** agrees, and departs to seek help.
5   While **A**'s away, **B** has some silly ideas about how to improve the situation: **B** tries to carry **C** down the hill, for example, then tries to light a fire to signal their distress.

Try it again with a twist

What if, instead of being three friends, **A** and **C** are guards taking prisoner **B** on a cross-country route to the nearest town, in wartime? When one of the guards breaks an ankle, it's a real problem for the other to decide what to do.

Things to do

Walking is one of the best ways of getting fit and losing weight.
But it has to be quite strenuous walking; not a ten-minute stroll.
Only an hour's sheer slog that gets your heart pumping faster
will really count. Get into the habit of going for walks and keep a
record of them. Take a camera along and keep an album of the
things you've seen.

Organise a competition among your friends. Each person
brings along a photograph of a local scene – not somewhere
obvious – and the winner is the one who can identify most of the
places.

Write a story beginning with the words: 'It was a beautiful
autumn day when I decided to go out for a walk'.

5   No Honour

A   Right, Bill. It's all perfectly straightforward, ain't it?
B   Sure.
A   OK. Repeat to me the details of how we do the job.
B   Right. We're after the safe at Underwood's handbag
    factory.
A   Which safe?
B   The one in the Director's office.
A   Manager's office, you berk!
B   Sorry, sorry. Right. It's dead easy. There's no
    nightwatchmen, no security guards.
A   Any sign of danger . . .
B   Any sign of danger, I whistle *Billericay Dickie*.
A   Where do you position yourself?

B On the bench by the wall. Under those trees. You get a good view from there, and I can look more natural, like.

A And if anyone comes . . .

B If anyone comes, I whistle *Billericay Dickie*.

A Time of kick off?

B Seven-thirty from here.

A Procedure, if anything goes wrong?

B Reverse fast down the mews and turn left into Broad Street.

A Right, you wally! It's a one-way street!

B Sorry.

A Golden Rule?

B Golden Rule – no violence.

Discuss

A is very opposed to violence, although he's a criminal. Some say that violence is becoming more common in this country. Think of some examples of violence in everyday life. Are there any times when violence is justified? What do you think are the worst examples of violence? Do you think videos, films and TV encourage violence? How? Does the violence you see on TV feel different to you as a spectator than it would in real life, if you happened to see something? How? And what effect does TV violence have on its audience? Do you approve of any of the following:

bullfights
boxing
foxhunting
corporal punishment
war – in certain circumstances.

The Plot Thickens

3 Characters:
A a burglar
B A's assistant
C a passer-by

The Outline

A and **B** plan to rob a factory. They know there's a lot of money in the manager's office. On the night of the burglary, **A** breaks in and **B** waits in the street keeping watch. **C** strolls up and starts to chat to **B**. **B** tries to get rid of **C**, finally panics and knocks **C** out. **A** returns and is furious.

A.   You've worked with **B** before and he/she has never let you down, though at times you think **B** is a bit slow. You hate violence and it's your proud boast that you've never had to resort to it in seven years' successful thieving.

B   You admire **A** and very much don't want to let **A** down in any way. So when **C** comes along you're really stuck: if **C** stays and **A** returns, **C** will realise what's going on and be a witness capable of recognising you both. That's what drives you to knock **C** out.

C.   You're taking an evening stroll when you come across this interesting-looking person and you feel like a chat. You live alone so you're a bit lonely. You breed champion bulldogs and canaries and you tell **B** all about the funny little habits of your favourite animals.

Suggested story-line

1   **A** and **B** plan the burglary, very professionally, with maps, etc. **A** does most of the thinking but **B** offers an idea or two as well.
2   The night of the robbery. **A** and **B** arrive at the factory, and **A** breaks in while **B** keeps watch.
3   **C** arrives and strikes up a conversation. **B** tries to get rid of **C** by dropping hints but it doesn't work.
4   Finally **B** has to knock **C** out. **A** returns and is furious with **B**. What should they do now? They argue about the possibilities.
5   **C** regains consciousness and **A** is very sympathetic and apologetic – but tries to explain that **B** can't be trusted.

Try it again with a twist

Suppose **C** turns out to be **A**'s cousin . . .

Things to do: Discuss

Do you think violence is an inevitable part of human nature?

Are boys and girls equally endowed with aggressive instincts, in your opinion? Does our society encourage boys and girls to express their aggressive instincts, or not? Make a list of the ways in which young people are pressurised either way. How might aggressive instincts be harmlessly exercised? Make a list of ideas for ways in which people could let off steam or release their anger without harming others.

Can you think of other ways in which we could re-organise our society so there is less violence? What general improvements might make a difference? (Think of education, weapons laws, leisure opportunities, improving the environment, etc.) Write an account of an ideal country where things are organised so that very little violence ever happens.

A Change of View

1   The Real Thing

A   Were you warm enough last night, love?

B   Yes, Mum.

A   Are you sure?

B   Of course I'm sure

A   Only I felt a bit chilly, myself. I hope I haven't taken cold.

B   But it's the middle of August.

A   You can't be too careful. August can be a really unhealthy month, sometimes.

B   What? With all this sun and fresh air?

A   I don't know. I feel this morning . . . as though I've got something on my chest, you know. Just a little tickle. And just a thought of soreness in my throat.

B   Where's my suede jacket, Mum?

A   Just have a look at my tongue, love. Does it look normal to you?

B   Ugh, put it away, Mum! I don't know what tongues are supposed to look like, anyway.

A   It feels a bit, you know . . . *furry*.

B   Well, perhaps you were a Teddy Bear in a previous existence.

The Plot Thickens

2 Characters:

A   a mother

B   her child

The Outline

Mum's a hypochondriac. **B** tries various ways of dealing with it – ignoring it, sympathising, etc. Then **B** falls ill, and whilst nursing him/her back to health **A** completely forgets about her own imaginary illnesses.

A. You always have a fear that you've got some deadly disease. You notice every little change in your bodily state, and become anxious immediately. But when **B** falls ill, you become so concerned you forget about yourself.

B. You accept your mum's hypochondria, though you're always trying in little ways to undermine it and persuade mum she's really fit as a fiddle. Then one day you get a really sore throat, and begin to ache and shiver all over . . .

Suggested story-line

1 **B** returns from school. **A** and **B** talk about the events of the day. **A** reports some new symptoms.
2 **B** starts to do his/her homework. **A** brings in a cup of tea. **B** has a sore throat and goes to bed early.
3 Next morning, **B** feels really ill, get up and collapses. **A** is very concerned.
4 **A** takes care of **B** and forgets about her own ailments.
5 **B**, feeling better by now, asks **A** how *she* feels – and **A** realises she's fit as a fiddle.

Try it again with a twist

What if it was the child who was the hypochondriac – and who fell ill?

Discuss

A person who always imagines that they are ill has what is called a psychosomatic illness. Another example of this might be a child who hates school and develops a violent stomach-ache when it's time for the new term to start. We often translate unhappiness or grief into some kind of pain or ache. Have you ever had any experience of this? What do you think are the requirements for a healthy life? How can the average person improve the quality of their life so they are healthier? If one's attitude of mind is also important for health, how can people relax more and avoid the stress that seems to be on the increase in modern life? What aspects of modern life seem to you to have increased people's anxieties and fears? (Compare our lives with the simpler lives of our ancestors who worked the fields.)

Things to do

Write a story entitled '*The Herb with Magic Powers*'.

Go to the library and find out which diseases have been conquered by modern medicine. Make a list of them. Which diseases have we still not developed a cure for? Organise a sponsored walk in aid of medical research.

2 Aprons Rule OK

A That was Mum. She just rang to say she'd be late home.

C What about our dinner, then?

A We make it ourselves, of course. Come on! Take those headphones off!

C Oh, Dad!

A I've always fancied having a crack at some of the recipes in this book. Let me see . . . how about 'Chilli con Carne'?

C But it's so hot today, Dad! Can't we have something cool?

A How about this, then? 'Lebanese Cucumber Soup'.

C What's that when it's at home?

A 'A delicious combination of yoghurt, cucumber, mint and herbs.' That's what it says.

C Sounds all right.

A Good. OK. This needs organisation. You go off down the garden and shoot a cucumber. And pick some mint.

C And what are you going to do?

A I'm going to take the yoghurt out of the fridge. An operation that calls for skill, daring and nerves of steel.

C Well, be careful you don't strain yourself. I'll go and get the mint and stuff.

A Now, what does it say in this book? . . . Wait a minute, that looks really delicious. 'Salmon Mousse with Waldorf Salad'. Maybe I'll try that tomorrow. And . . . hey, 'Summer Pudding'. Absolutely delicious. I wonder if I could make that at the weekend? The trouble with Gillian is that she never has enough time to devote to these things. Now then . . . 'Lebanese Cucumber Soup' . . . We need a dash of tarragon vinegar. Wonder if we've got any? Let's see . . . wine vinegar . . . malt vinegar . . . hooray! Tarragon vinegar!

C Dad! Here's the cucumber, and there's the mint. Now can I go back to Elvis Costello, please?

A You certainly cannot. That's not a cucumber, it's a courgette, you idiot!

Discuss

Do you think a woman's place is in the home? If a woman casts off her housewife role, goes out to work and is a success, she will obviously benefit. How? And how will her family and friends benefit? If nobody in a family really wants to do the domestic work – cooking, cleaning and shopping – how should it be organised? Do you think people (men *and* women) are still prejudiced about what a woman's role should be? Think of examples of this prejudice. Do men suffer from similar prejudices: being expected to be strong, fearless, unemotional, good at mending things etc.? Think of examples. What are the best ways of breaking down these prejudices?

The Plot Thickens

3 Characters:
A Dad
B Mum
C son/daughter

The Outline

Both parents are wage-earners. Then Dad loses his job. He decides to learn the household skills. So, helped by the family, he learns to cook, sew etc. – and turns out to be better at them than Mum.

A.   What would your reaction be to losing your job? You might try at first to get another, but you're forced in the end to put your energies into household skills. At first you're awkward at them, but gradually you really begin to enjoy them.

B.   You're doing very well at work. At the very moment Dad loses his job, you get promoted. You gladly teach Dad to do the household tasks – after all, you've had to fit them in your spare time up till now. As a result, you get a lot more rest, so you're delighted.

C.   You're upset by Dad losing his job, and you're amused at the idea of his becoming cook and housekeeper. You thought Dad was too set in his ways to do any such thing – so your view of Dad really changes.

Suggested story-line

1   The family tea. **B** comes home and tells **C** she's been promoted, then **A** comes home and announces he's lost his job.
2   **A**'s been looking for new work for weeks now, without success. He therefore decides it would be a better idea for him to become a house-husband.
3   **A** teaches **B** to cook, starting with simple things like omelettes. **C** watches and makes helpful/jokey comments.
4   **C**'s birthday tea. Dad's made a cake, scones, and a wonderful trifle. And he's knitted **C** a jumper, too!

Try it again with a twist

Suppose Mum became jealous and insecure at the thought of Dad taking over her traditional work . . .

Things to do

Learn to cook. Take an evening course if you can't do it at school. Or teach yourself from cookery books. Keep a record of your progress.

Imagine a boy has invited a girl to dinner, and he's decided to dazzle and impress her by cooking a very ambitious meal. But luck is against him and everything goes wrong. Write an account of his evening. How might it all end? Happily? Unhappily?

3 Smile, Please

24 Leafield Drive
Podsworth
Hants.
4th February

Dear Lesley,

I've landed a fantastic job – I'm so lucky. It's just what I've always wanted: a photographer's assistant. I'll learn all the tricks of the trade: how to use cameras, light meters etc. And how to develop and print film in the darkroom. I'm so excited, I can hardly wait to start!

Adam (that's the photographer) also goes on trips around the country because apart from doing portraits, wedding photos etc., he's a landscape photographer. So I'll be doing quite a bit of travelling, too. He's a fantastic guy – very nice and friendly.

I can't quite say the same for his wife, though. She's called Caroline, and when I was first introduced she was a bit frosty. Since then she's give me a few really dirty looks. The thing is, she used to help Adam but now I've come along I suppose she might begin to feel a bit left out. Anyway, whatever the reason, I'm definitely not her favourite person at the moment.

Still, everything else is fine, and I'll be able to pay you that money I owe you really soon. I'm so sorry you've had to wait so long for it.

Yours sincerely,
Billie

The Plot Thickens

3 Characters
A   photographer
B   his assistant
C   his wife

The Outline

A photographer works hard and gets a new assistant. But soon afterwards strange things start to happen. Some films of empty landscapes show shadowy figures when they're developed, and a lot of the machinery in the dark room develops electrical faults.

A.   Most of your work is photographing people in the studio. But you also go on trips and photograph the landscape. You need an assistant to help develop and print the films, to keep the studio clean, and help with the books.

B.   You're very glad to get this job, because you're terribly hard up and you've been looking for work for months. You're very keen to do well and you hope that the photographer and his wife will like you.

C.   You don't take to the new assistant, yet you have to admit there are no real reasons for your dislike. But when strange things begin to happen, you begin to suspect the assistant of having some kind of psychic powers. You are afraid and try to persuade your husband to get rid of **B**. But he thinks you're just being superstitious and jealous.

Suggested story-line

1   **A** and **C** discuss the volume of work and decide **A** needs an assistant.
2   **B** arrives for the first day's work and is shown round. **B** cleans the studio, watches **A** developing a film, works well.
3   **A** discovers the developed film with the shadowy figures. **B** arrives and is also mystified by this. They discuss possible explanations: something wrong with the film, the camera, the light, etc.
4   After **B** has gone, **A** tells **C** about it. **C** is very superstitious and is scared, and eventually begins to wonder if it might be

B's influence.

5   **A** and **C** argue about whether to ask **B** to leave or not.

Try it again with a twist

Suppose the photographer's wife began to feel strange pains in her head and the doctor cannot find an explanation for this mystery illness.

Discuss

The photographer's wife felt sure that the new assistant was the source of the psychic disturbance. Do you know anybody who has extra-sensory powers: who shares telepathic thoughts or gets glimpses of what will happen in the future? What are your views about the paranormal? (ghosts, telepathy, pre-cognition, etc.). Do you believe in ghosts, do you think they might exist only in the imagination of those who see them, or do you dismiss the whole subject as nonsense?

Things to do

Go to the library and find out all you can about the Paranormal (ghosts, poltergeists, telepathy, pre-cognition, extra-sensory perception etc.). A good book is Brian Inglis's *Natural and Supernatural*.

Write a ghost story.

Ask everybody you know to tell you their own experience of the supernatural things that have happened to them or their friends. Make a collection of such stories.

4 Nosey Parker

Postman	A registered letter for you today, Mrs Parker.
Annie	Thank you very much. Was that an air letter I just saw you delivering next door?
Postman	Can't say as I remember.
Annie	I expect it was from their friends in America. You know they've got some friends in California, don't you?
Postman	Have they?
Annie	Oh yes. He's something big in the University. He's a professor, I believe.
Postman	Just sign here for the registered letter, please.
Annie	Right you are. But then, they're a very clever family altogether, aren't they? Ben's doing eight 'O' levels – just imagine!
Postman	Ah, he's a sharp one, all right.
Annie	Oh, they're marvellous neighbours, altogether. Christine always makes sure I'm all right for jam and jelly and whenever she makes a pie she always brings me a piece.
Postman	Right you are, Mrs Parker . . .
Annie	And Brian's very patient, too. He made me some lovely shelves last year. And he puts up the frames for my runner beans for me.
Postman	Oh yes . . .
Annie	I think I do try his patience at times, but he's very good to me.
Postman	Well, I must be going.
Annie	Oooh, they've had some terrible trouble, though, that family.
Postman	You'll have to excuse me, Mrs . . .
Annie	Did you ever hear about the time Brian was stung by a swarm of bees?
Postman	No.

Annie	And then there was that time when the owls built their nest in his aerial.
Postman	I'm sorry, Mrs Parker, but I really must go. The mail must get through, you know.
Annie	Yes, yes, dear of course. Are you feeling quite all right? You do look a little pale and peaky . . .
Postman	Goodbye!

The Plot Thickens

4 Characters:
A a neighbour
B father
C mother
D child

The Outline

A nosey neighbour keeps coming round. She gossips a lot and is always trying to find out what's going on. Mum tolerates her, Dad ignores her. The child teases her. Then one day she falls and breaks her hip. From then on, she needs help . . .

A. You're rather lonely and you really like the family next door. You want to know all about them and you ask lots of questions without realising you're being nosey.

B. You think the neighbour is just a nuisance and you wish that **A** would keep her curiosity to herself. You like your home life to be peaceful and quiet.

C You tolerate the neighbour because you feel sorry for her: she's lonely and after all, it doesn't hurt to be kind to people. All the same, you can't help being irritated at times.

D. You think the neighbour's a great laugh. You're always poking fun at her and half the time she doesn't even realise it. But when she's injured you begin to see her as someone worthy of your pity and kindness.

Suggested story-line

1 Tea-time: **B** comes home from work, **D** from school. The family's enjoying a cosy evening when **A** comes round with

her constant questions.

2   When **A**'s gone, Dad gets quite angry about her. The others try to pacify him.

3   One day **D** is walking past **A**'s house when she/he hears a faint call for help. **D** finds **A** lying at the bottom of the stairs, fetches Mum and Dad to help, and they take her to hospital.

4   When **A** comes out of hospital, the family rallies round and helps her. Even Dad is prepared to help, making her a little bedside table.

5   The family discuss her, once they're back home. They've come to feel rather differently about her since her accident.

Try it again with a twist

Suppose **A** actually died as a result of the fall, and the verdict was that she wasn't receiving enough care and attention from her friends and neighbours.

Discuss

The family found their neighbour irritating. What sort of things irritate you? Do you think you are a tolerant person, or not? Which faults do you think should be tolerated? Is it sometimes better to blow your top and let off steam when somebody irritates you? Some families often shout at each other, but some never have rows. Which suits you best? Why? If you feel irritable and can't let off steam, what's the best thing to do?

Things to do

Write some comic poems (they don't have to rhyme) in the character of a gossip.

   Get in touch with your local hospital and find out what you can do to help the patients there: maybe you could put on a show for them, or collect books and magazines for them.

   Write an account of a time when you were ill or injured (whether you had to go into hospital or not). Include details of how you felt and how people's behaviour towards you changed.

5   Windfalls and Bruises

B   Arthur? Arthur!

A   What is it, dear? I'm busy.

B   Busy doing what?

A   Watching *Yes, Minister*.

B   Never mind that! I need help!

A   What's the matter?

B   Water's pouring through the ceiling, Arthur!

A   Oh God. I'm coming . . . Good Lord! What on earth caused that, I wonder?

B   Don't just stand there – go and find a plastic bucket.

A   There's one in that cupboard . . . Here you are.

B   Where can it be coming from?

A   I don't know. It's a blocked-off sort of roof space above this room. There's no way I can get up there to have a look without making a hole in the ceiling.

B   Well, what can we do?

A   Much better to wait till morning and call a plumber . . . except that we can't afford it.

B   Oh, Arthur! You're hopeless.

A   I'll think of something, love. Maybe I'll win the pools. Then we'll be able to afford two plumbers.

B   Never mind two plumbers! If you won the pools we could have a new house!

The Plot Thickens

4 Characters:
A   man who wins
B   his wife
C   a jealous workmate
D   a greedy workmate

The Outline

A man wins the pools. He tries to carry on his normal life but finds that his wife and his workmates treat him differently. So he gives the money away.

A. You've led a fairly ordinary life and you like it that way. You get on well with your workmates, you enjoy a peaceful home life and when all that changes you become very unhappy.

B. You're very shocked at the thought of all that money – but then you begin to fantasise about all the marvellous things you could buy – the fast cars, the fur coats etc.

C. When **A** wins the pools you feel very jealous. You desperately need money because your wife's mother is ill and your children want to go on to further education. You think **A** will get big-headed as a result of his win. You feel rather sour about it.

D. When **A** wins all that money you see your big chance. You've always been **A**'s best mate – so why shouldn't you get your share? You set about trying to wheedle your way into **A**'s plans.

Suggested story-line

1 **A** and **B** are chatting over tea when the phone rings and **A** is told he's won £100,000. They are amazed.
2 Next day **A** tells his mates at work. They all go out for a drink to celebrate.
3 At home, **B** starts to let her imagination run riot as to all the things she wants. **A** is rather surprised by her greed.
4 At work, **C** begins to make sour and envious remarks. **A** has lunch with **D** who dismisses **C** as jealous, and tries to flatter **A** and ingratiate himself.
5 **A** announces to his wife that he's given the lot to Oxfam. Then, next day at work, he tells his workmates.

Try it again with a twist

Suppose **A** decides that the best thing to do is spend it all as quickly as possible . . .

Discuss

Do you think that Arthur was right to give his money away? Or was he unadventurous and unimaginative? Do you think success or good fortune always spoils people? Do you envy people who are rich, or beautiful, or highly intelligent? Which of these would your most envy?

Things to do

Imagine you're Arthur's wife. Write some extracts from a diary she might have kept, from just before the big win until Arthur gives the money away. Show clearly her fears, hopes, anxieties.

Imagine you've just won £100,000. Write an account of what you would do and how your life would change. Do you think it would change your personality as well?

Is there anything to be said for not being rich? Does the simple life have any virtues? Write a dialogue between a rich man and an ordinary farm worker who meet one lunchtime in a country pub.